HMS LITTLE FOX

Books by Lee Harwood

POETRY
title illegible
The Man with Blue Eyes
The White Room
Landscapes
The Sinking Colony
Penguin Modern Poets 19 (with John Ashbery & Tom Raworth)
Freighters
H.M.S. Little Fox
Boston-Brighton
Old Bosham Bird Watch
Wish you were here (with Antony Lopez)
All the Wrong Notes
Faded Ribbons
Monster Masks
Crossing the Frozen River: selected poems
Rope Boy to the Rescue
In the Mists: mountain poems
Morning Light
Evening Star
Collected Poems *
Selected Poems *
The Orchid Boat

PROSE
Captain Harwood's Log of Stern Statements and Stout Sayings
Wine Tales: Un Roman Devin (with Richard Caddel)
Dream Quilt: 30 assorted stories
Assorted Stories : prose works
Not the Full Story: 6 Interviews (with Kelvin Corcoran) *

TRANSLATIONS
Tristan Tzara – *Cosmic Realities Vanilla Tobacco Dawnings*
Tristan Tzara – *Destroyed Days, a selection of poems 1943-1955*
Tristan Tzara – *Selected Poems*
Tristan Tzara – *Chanson Dada: Selected Poems*
Tristan Tzara – *The Glowing Forgotten: A Selection of Poems*

(* Shearsman titles)

HMS LITTLE FOX

LEE HARWOOD

SHEARSMAN LIBRARY

Second Edition.
Published in the United Kingdom in 2018 by
The Shearsman Library
an imprint of Shearsman Books
50 Westons Hill Drive
Emersons Green
BRISTOL
BS16 7DF

Shearsman Books Ltd Registered Office
30–31 St. James Place, Mangotsfield, Bristol BS16 9JB
(this address not for correspondence)

www.shearsman.com

ISBN 978-1-84861-593-9

First published by Oasis Books, London, 1975
with ISBN 0 903375 22 2

Copyright © Lee Harwood, 1975
Copyright © The Estate of Lee Harwood, 2018
All rights reserved

The right of Lee Harwood to be identified as the author of this work has been asserted by his Estate in accordance with Section 77 of the Copyright, Designs and Patents Act 1988.

*

The hieroglyph of the Egyptian goddess Hathor on page 7 (and elsewhere in 'The Long Black Veil') was drawn by Peter Bailey and the drawing of Anubis on page 32 is by Ian Robinson.

The five photographs of ships that introduce each section of the book are from the old postcard collection belonging to the author.

The 'Five postcards to Alban Berg' have been set to music by Herman Weiss under the same title.

Contents

The Long Black Veil: A Notebook 1970-72
    Preface   9
    Books 1 to 12   11

Qasída Island 1971-72
    Qasída   43
    One, Two, Three   47
    Blue Enamel Letter J   51
    New Year   54
    With a Photo by John Walsh   56
    Five Postcards to Alban Berg   58

'Inside the harm is a clearing…'   63

The Big Chop 1969-70
    North   73
    Night Ferry   74
    Country Diary Continued   75
    Today   76
    S…… – Hebrew for 'Beautiful'   77
    Brooklyn   78
    Little Lord Fauntleroy Meets The Secret Garden   79

H.M.S. Little Fox 1967-68
    The Situation   85
    Dawn of the Monsters   87
    Chemical Days   88
    The Revisitation   89
    Dazzle   90
    Forestry Work No. 1   91
    Love in the Organ Loft   92
    The Nine Death Ships   95

A Note by the Author   98
A Note from the Publisher   99

THE LONG BLACK VEIL :

a notebook 1970-72

> *things have ends (or scopes) and beginnings. To know what precedes   and what follows will assist yr / comprehension of process*

Ezra Pound – *Canto 77*

> *In the Congo what joy could I take in gathering unknown flowers with no one to whom to give them?*

André Gide – *Journals*, 31 March 1930

Preface

How to accept
this drift

the move   not mapped
nor clear other than in
its existence

a year passed
I think of you
it's early on a sunny morning in June
and think of your thinking of me
possible

How do we live with this?
yet live with this

What have we *left*
from all *this*?

      'Concepts promise protection
from experience.
              The spirit does
not dwell in concepts. Oh Jung.'
          (Joanne Kyger – *Desecheo Notebook*)

two years passed   'Oh Jung'
the cycle not repeated
only the insistence

The story is that, when a child, Borges used to come to his father. His father would have a number of coins that he would place on his desk one by one, one on top of the other. To be brief – the stack of coins is an image of how our memory distorts and simplifies events the farther we move from them. The first coin is the actual event, the next coin is the event recreated in the mind, the memory, the next coin is a recreation of the first recreation, etc., etc.,...

But what of the essence of this? 'Oh Jung's' insistences. The Sufi story of the famous River that tried to cross the desert, but only crossed the sands as water 'in the arms of the wind', nameless but

Book One

the soft dawn   it's light
I mean your body   and how I ache now
yes, tremble

        the words?   how can they…

somehow the raven flying through endless skies
that ache too much   the unbearable distance
borne

Across the valley the sun catches the white silos
of these scattered farms
Up on the ridge

I mean following the creek…

As we lie in each other
dazed and hanging like birds on the wind

your body, yes   I'm talking about it
at last   I mean this *is* the discovery
Need I list the items?

On your way from the thorn tree to the house
you stop and half turn
to tell me…
that doesn't matter
but your look
and this picture I have
and at this distance

I have this now
I have what I have
        in my hands

dawn – light – body – words – raven – skies – ache – distance – valley – sun – silos – farms – ridge – creek – each other – birds – wind

The Flight – BA 591

Book Two

Baseball in Central Park.
Anti-war parade on 5th Avenue.
The Egyptian rooms in the Metropolitan.
Reading Gide's *Journals* in my room.

On the bus : the green Catskills. large black birds standing in the grass. wild blue iris in the swamps. two woodchucks. two rabbits. If other men's shoes fit, wear 'em.

We swim naked in the pool at night. The stars so bright. The hot night, the crickets and frogs singing. I hold you to me in a small room – the night air so heavy. Inside 'the dream' …

A farm dog barks somewhere across the valley.

The bright greens of the woods, the sun streaming down through the branches. The crashings of a chicken hawk suddenly startled and flying up through the branches to the safety of the sky again. The rain that increases and

    thunder in the distance
    the air heavy
    and the valley white with mist

    our bodies wet

As dawn breaks
we wake
and make love
again
the sky grey outside
and the birds singing

The sun comes up
You rise and make coffee
The woods so green

We go back to bed and

I can hear your footsteps
going about the house
doing things
while I sit by the window
of this upstairs room

the birds singing
in the heavy afternoon
the muffled sounds of a t.v.
downstairs

that I want you
this is why

I will call anything that goes on in my head 'a dream', whether it be thoughts or imaginings, day-dreams or sleep dreams. They all give pictures of 'the possible', and that is exactly their value.

the two warships ploughed out to sea
waves flowed between them
as though dolphins lovingly touched each hull
in turn   No flecks of dust on the captain's
fine uniform   All the brass polished

Not the first   but one of many
such expeditions

Book Three

1:00 pm, check into the hotel. It has two rooms and a bar. The town has two stores, three bars, a post office, church, gas station, fire station, and a small country library. People drive into town in their pick-up trucks, but it's not *that* 'country'.

Evening time out on the front porch step, smoking a cigar, watching the cars and people pass. Night bugs flying round the lights. Young men driving in pegs, putting up tents back of the fire station ready for the weekend 'Fire Department Chicken Fry'. The hot heavy night bringing the thunder and warm rain. Go to bed, the noise of passing trucks and the juke-box downstairs.

The fascination with *this* formality, *this* ritual.

Woken up early in the morning by the thunder, and rain beating on the tin roof of the porch. When I get up the air so soft and sweet. The square and hillsides a soft white with the fine mist. In the bar local farmers and workers from the nearby steel mills talking – '…a nigger wench, not a nigger woman…' As I leave the sun breaks through on to the lush greenness of this valley.

Walk up the ridge west of the town – the minnows darting in the creek. The rock bed, and the currents there. The smell of young ferns as I walk up the hill through the beech woods.

Go up to the wild strawberry patch again, squat down and eat some. Continue up along the road, the pine woods by the crest of the ridge   'see for miles'

You walk through the door
No, now you stop your car in a small town square
I get up from the porch step and greet you
This is all 'country manners'

There's no steamer bringing you to me
up-river at the hill-station
No long white dress on the verandah

It is...
I hold you.	Isn't this enough?
The feel of your breasts
     beneath your loose white shirt

'It was used by the commentator of the Himyarite Ode, either at first hand or through the medium of Hamdani's *Iklil*. We may regard it, like the commentary itself, as a historical romance in which most of the characters and some of the events are real, adorned with fairy-tales, fictitious verses, and such entertaining matter as a man of learning and storyteller by trade might naturally be expected to introduce. Among the few remaining Muhammadan authors who bestowed special attention on the Pre-Islamic period of South Arabian history, I shall mention here only Hamza of Isfahan, the eighth book of whose *Annals* (finished in 961 A.D.) provides a useful sketch, with brief chronological details, of the Tubba's or Himyarite kings of Yemen.'
                       (R. A. Nicholson – *A Literary History of The Arabs*)

The small town set in a valley winding between ridges,
the lush green, the white mist at dawn,
the creek bed almost dry,
white scattered boulders and the willows.
The meadows so deep, and floating on their surface
the yellow and orange flowers.
The cool beech woods on late afternoons.
You melt into this landscape
and this only a description of my love for you

At the hill-station   all the bearers fled

The delighted naturalist was left unconcerned
carefully placing his specimens in the black metal box

'…and when he spoke about it to his friends they smiled and said they found the comparison *odd*, but they immediately dropped the subject and went on to talk about something else. Hebdomeros concluded from this that perhaps they had not really understood what he meant, and he reflected on the difficulty of making oneself understood when one's thoughts reached a certain height or depth. 'It's strange,' Hebdomeros was thinking, "as for me, the very idea that something had escaped my understanding would keep me awake at nights, whereas people in general are not in the least perturbed when they see or read or hear things they find completely obscure."'

(Giorgio de Chirico – *Hebdomeros*)

Book Four

We choose our condition

the sun shines
the warmth and softness of your flesh
'belly to belly' (like the song says)

The air so clear up on the ridge
this light
and then looking down to the valley

'our condition chooses us'
she says

In the morning we go for a drive, buy cakes and milk, and picnic by the creek. The afternoon spent in the meadow. In the evening we make love in the room.

the sun glittering   through the glass
scattering rainbows on the walls and ceiling
the soft turf beneath the trees outside
your room where we lie naked
with our love

the country music plays
the words sung
'Palms of victory, crowns of glory.
 Palms of victory I shall wear.'

…felt so good this morning – as though I woke up beside you.

Book Five: Canadian Days

On the Northlands train from Toronto up to North Bay, Cochrane, and Kapuskasing. Then bus onto Hearst ('Moose Capital of the North'), and a jeep ride out to Jogues.
The night before the train full of drunks and bear hunters. Ridiculous. 'No guffing'.

And today early morning, the grey dawn. The 'towns' we stop at just a collection of huts scattered at random around the rail halt and a dirt road. And then the bush again. Heavy streams and rivers, and the forest cluttered with dead and fallen trees. The occasional windswept meadow, a grey weathered farmhouse deserted, fallen apart. Nothing. The bleak empty plain, marsh, lakes, the crowded conifer woods, a single silver birch in the middle of this.

The Northlands. The watery sunlight on dirt roads. The dull green country. Hardly any flowers to be seen.

At night the stars brighter than I'd ever seen them, and the curtains of light, the Aurora Borealis. This brightness dazzling, but it's with you that I want it.

It is the surface
your eyes
The foresters tramp in weary
Driven into a corner (so to speak)
to say this
I hold your head between my hands
your eyes

In the morning sitting on the front step, everything so calm and still. The warm sun, and a total quiet only broken by the bark of the ravens. The vast blue sky, and the forest stretching off on all sides. The long straight white dirt roads with a line of telegraph poles along side, and then the forest enclosing them on either side.

Book Six

The questions of complexity

On Gide's death Mr. Forster said – 'I realized more clearly how much he had got out of life, and had managed to transmit through his writings. Not life's greatness – greatness is a nineteenth century perquisite, a Goethean job. But life's complexity, and the delight, the difficulty, the duty of registering that complexity and of conveying it.'

The distinctions

'Oh, Jung' (1875-1961) on 'Marriage...' (1925)

The container *and* the contained
not *or*

one within the other
a continual shifting   and that both ways
– more a flow – from the simplicity to the complexity,
'unconscious' to conscious,
                           and then back again?
and the move always with difficulty, and pain   a pleasure

not so much a repetition
but a moving around a point, a line
– like a backbone – and that too moving
(on)

                    yang and yin
                    light and dark

An island set among islands
and that no answer
But the need there –
somehow to have all one's hopes there,
to see and touch, to be wholly in one place.
Yet over the horizon   as real as any…
the ghosts
and them always moving

BEFORE COMPLETION   Wei Chi / 64
But if the little fox, after nearly completing the crossing
Gets his tail in the water,
There is nothing that would further.

                    in the half light…
A minotaur? a cat? tiger?   Her face
a metamorphosis   seen   at once   many times.
Our powers generating…
We touch, hold, and caress ourself

A bird flying high in the sky
above the clouds, and below them
an ocean, and a ship moving there.

'Such thoughts were very far from Julien's mind. His love was still another name for ambition. It meant for him the joy of possessing so beautiful a woman, when he himself was a poor, unhappy creature whom men despised. His acts of adoration, and his rapture at the sight of his mistress's charms, ended by reassuring Madame de Rênal on the question of the difference in their ages. Had she possessed a little of that practical knowledge of the world which in the most civilized countries a woman of thirty has had at her disposal for a number of years already, she might have trembled for the duration of a love which apparently only existed on surprise and the transports of gratified self-esteem.'

                    (Stendhal – *Le rouge et le noir*)

Book Seven

My stomach   burns   Coming to you

How will…?

The peaceful and flowering public gardens,
the smell of the ocean again
So much tied in such sites
of past pleasures

Stepping into the new   always   with you

A low haze beyond the harbour's mouth

I am full and happy   now   at your side

…we finally begin to fall asleep as dawn comes, as a single whippoorwill starts to sing…

we wake, and make love. Outside a grey sea mist fills the woods. Later, standing alone in these woods waiting for her, not knowing how… this journey today so far from

The tricks are pulled

     blue skies flash across the screen

The falsity when anything becomes a symbol

You are lowered   very gently
into the waiting boat alongside

Much later   ashore on this island,
where tears rarely happen...

You are away there on other continents
So hard – 'It is hard to stand firm in the middle'
– waiting   for that lightness, that ease
of movement

The freighter was anchored in the middle of the bay with a full head of steam up. As the launch approached

In the Museum of Fine Arts, Boston –

> *Mycerinus and his queen, Khamerernebty II*
> slate. fourth dynasty (2613-2494 B.C.)
> (The Pharaoh Mycerinus also known as Menkaure.)

In the Egyptian Museum, Cairo –

> *Mycerinus triad : Mycerinus, Hathor, and the*
> *personification of the 'Dog' nome.*
> slate. fourth dynasty.
> (The personification of the 'Dog' district
> (nome) is a woman.)

the tenderness. They stand facing us, she to his left, her right arm around his waist, her left hand resting on his left upper arm.

Horus, Hathor, Anubis.

Horus – the falcon-headed god, the sun.

Hathor – the cow-headed goddess, the sky.

Anubis – the jackal-headed god, the guardian of the dead.

Horus, the rising sun, enters Hathor, the sky.
Obvious enough.

Doors flung open, a clear blue day outside, cactus, sage brush, and the yellow desert ochre, and the blue sky.   New Mexico.

Horus, son of Osiris, a falcon, whose two eyes are the sun and the moon, and whose breath is the cooling north wind.

Hathor, the cow, the sky goddess, stars on her belly, the sun between her horns, guardian of the Western Mountain, goddess of the copper mines of Sinai, of a woman's love and joy, of perfumes and spices, identified by the Greeks as Aphrodite. The mother who gives birth to Ra, the sun, at dawn. The destroyer on whose back Ra rides through the sky.

Anubis, the jackal, guardian of the desert cemeteries, master of embalmment, who oversees the weighing of each heart.

'a god is power personified… In Egypt…'

No godhead, no gospel, but 'a multiplicity of approaches', each in its own right, each immanent in nature.

Book Eight : England

So much either side of the immediate
though at its height – the love ecstasy
of the 'now' – it is only the immediate,
God's face.
(the Sufi poet, Ibn 'Arabi, writes of this)
God's face is the face of your lover.

I love you

the sky is full of wheeling gulls
Do I ask too much?
– the sea crashing white on the shingle –
that I'm torn apart each time you leave

the white buildings
the green sea and hills behind the town,
like some giant sandwich
and our love in the filling of it

You wheel above me

such whiteness

Christ, that I love you

how to deal with this?

I wait for you
not passively   but
I wait for you

My heart weeps

Who would ever have thought I'd write that?
'My heart weeps'?

'You must try, Psyche, to use up all your facility against an obstacle; face the granite, rouse yourself against it, and for a while despair. See your vain enthusiasms and your frustrated aims fall away. Perhaps you lack sufficient wisdom yet to prefer your will to your ease. You find that stone too hard, you dream of the softness of wax and the obedience of clay? Follow the path of your aroused thought and you will soon meet this infernal inscription: *There is nothing so beautiful as that which does not exist.*'
(Paul Valéry – *Concerning Adonis*)

Not a climbing, but a moving across the surface in a certain way, as though a soaking into the grain, what was there all the time, though never fully realised.

As though a monster haunts us – continually aroused at each 'wrong' word, each 'wrong' action, and roaring out from its darkness to terrorize us again. A giant and indestructible serpent filled with anger and venom, nightmare.

'Each single angel is terrible.' (Rilke)

Summer. The water meadows at dusk. The willows and long grass either side of the winding river, now only seen as a smooth black surface, the flow imperceptible. The buttercups indistinguishable in the growing darkness. Only the sound of your feet on the narrow gravel path. A cuckoo in a nearby spinney. The swallows out hunting. Across the fields the dim outline of the town – a clock strikes the hour, maybe in the church or the marketplace.

Book Nine

Today, lying on the grass in the park
by your house
                    We were very close
Your husband, your children, you go
about your duties, you love
and care for them

Yes.

you there
me here

sometimes it's an ocean
spread between our bodies
sometimes only a matter of
yards across a carpeted room

you sit there
I sit here
there are people around us

the luxury
of setting eyes on you

You walk by my side through the park
what luxury
the

the cars the planes
the absurd mechanics
when all I want
is to walk up the hill to you

the silly girls clatter round
while you – the only woman I know,
the only woman I want –
are kept so securely from me
and at such a distance

a fierce wind tugs at the town
while I walk up the hill
and you on the other shore
while the sea bursts on this shore

there is a fine rain – I repeat myself –
it's night   there is a wind
To answer to…?
when our world turns in us
dazzling
That hand offered us when the clouds part

'No, it's real,
it's what I feel.'
              (*The Soft Machine*)

The pride. Being with you, knowing very simply where I'm going, where I stand, of being able to put aside all the half-things and live with one sure knowledge of what matters, what is.

'…an ease in the air around us that we can spread into … and ideas are like stars instead of gravity – we're not held by them by their necessities.'
            (*your letter*)

Book Ten

The rain falling
you could be driving a car now
somewhere

You drive the car and my hand rests on your shoulder
the radio is playing
the rain is beating on the car roof
and the road is a brilliant black

the honour of you
'I am honoured' someone says

that I should cry now

we all know what this means
and there's no need for any rich details

when John said 'from egotistical to egocentric'
he was right about the process
there's no cause for shame

and the 'honour'?

the word grows emptier the farther it moves
from the flesh
while *my* honour lives in your flesh

'You're your own train, you got your own track, and you can go anywhere.'
(Fielding Dawson quoting Charles Olson in
The Black Mountain Book*)*

But you the ground,
earth I want,
the place

the luxury of it
to hold my reality in my arms

the touch
of it
you
the feel of you
so much now

Book Eleven

Is it the Rilkean dream or 'home' we come to?
At dusk the skyline obscure.
Yes and No.

Many pictures – the surface apparently the same.
A series of events, but the marks they leave
varying.   Things happen, have qualities.

And ahead?

The mountains, the wind, the sea   are there
we move through them, across their surfaces

like a moving hunter

On a 'threshold'?   in the open
dazzled by the sunlight, and 'nervous',

but moving – and that with care.
No end.

But the quality

The dreams do happen –
and there is no 'home' we come to
– but on this earth, and open to its powers

A recognition of the ghosts that guide us. The dead watching over us, surrounding us with a tenderness – as though they were gravity – they hold us, their arms around us, however we move.

And Anubis guiding the dead through their journey.

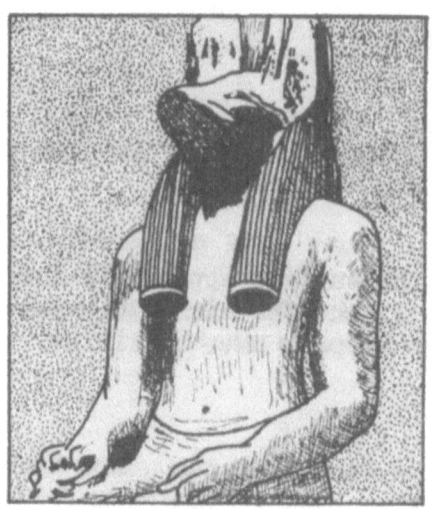

Before the tribunal of Osiris, Anubis, the jackal-headed god, watches over the weighing of the dead man's heart – the heart in one scale, and in the other an ostrich feather, symbol of Ma'at, the goddess of truth. And if the heart is truthful the dead man is led up to Osiris by Anubis and becomes Osiris, god of the dead, of the under world – that is, of the earth beneath our feet.

Book Twelve : California Journal

the eucalyptus groves on the mountain sides the road cuts through – no – follows the contour obediently. The coast…

the heat and wetness of us

later alone on the beach … the sandpipers rush about, following each wave out, picking the sand. The gulls

...through the barrier. 'That isn't pain, it's something else.'

driving through the mountains. San Anselmo. San Rafael. The redwoods. The ease of walking in the hot sun in California down a dirt path laughing, ordering milk-shakes, and watching the traffic pass. Of being totally in one place. The dry mountains around us. Nowhere else

At night the smell of orange blossom at the post-office

In the bar I talked with this man passing through town about Union matters.

'...For Beauty's nothing
but the beginning of Terror we're still just able to bear,
and we adore it so because it serenely
disdains to destroy us. Each single angel is terrifying.

Ein jeder Engel ist schrecklich.'
(Rilke – *Duino Elegies 1*)

walk the length of the beach as far as the rocks watching the small and large sandpipers. Orange butterflies glide above the parking lot.

when we're together the time always so short. The minutes counted and noted down. And around these times the long hours of waiting.

that hot surface where our bodies meet, press together – 'a melting spot'.

she tells me of

                              the tearing

                                                              leaving

                    the only woman

We drive up into the mountains behind the beach. Muir Woods. Mount Tamalpais. The air so clear and sweet. On the short turf… her laughing. She looks so beautiful.

In the evening in the room…

Making love, the final blocks clear. My body taken into her body completely, and then her body into my body.

In that place the ease there

more beautiful than ever, her black hair so thick and rich

She anoints my wrists

the anointment a ritual like the sweetening of the body before burial, before our parting. My not realising the completeness of this until now.

In the distance the mountains – the dream echoed again and again in many parts, in many places. An antelope (not understanding this animal) lies down exhausted yet calm. Some form of quietness.

The ritual of – repeated again – No. We make love – to each other – in turn. The body glowing, dizzy, … walking through clouds. The faces transformed again.

She accepts the objects – the stone, the orange blossom.
She gives the objects – the whittled twig, the dried seed pod.

She puts the bead bracelet around my wrist

      lie naked upon the bed.

       § § §

Qasída Island

1971-72

Qasída

it's *that*
the quiet room
the window open, trees outside
'blowing' in the wind.
the colour is called green.
the sky.
the colour is called blue.
(sigh)   the crickets singing

windows open.   You move…
No, not so much a moving
but the artificiality of containment
in one skin. 'No man an island' (ha-ha Buddha)
…lonesome, huh?

THE music, THE pictures
(go walkabout)
Small wavy lines on the horizon

somewhere over the distant horizon
the distant city (I hadn't thought of this,
but pull it in) and you

the children are sleeping
and you're probably sitting in the big chair
reading or sewing something
It's quarter past nine
I find you beautiful

○

the words come slowly. No…
your tongue   the lips moving
the words reach out –
crude symbols – the hieroglyphs
sounds, *not* pictures

the touching beyond this –
I touch you

in the water
as though I'm in you

that joy
and skipping in the street
the children hanging on our arms

◯

You know… – the signals (on the horizon?)
'blocked off'   the ships at night
keep moving

these clear areas beyond the clutter
that clearing

on summer nights as we lie together…

there are green trees in the street
yes, there is the whole existence of
our bodies lying naked together
the two skins touching
the coolness of your breasts
the touch

The setting…
it doesn't really matter
We know
So much goes on around us

on the quay they're playing music
we'll eat and dance there,
when the wind gets cold
we'll put our sweaters on
it's that simple, really…

◯

...the dry fields
Up on the mountain sides
white doves (of course) glide
on the air-currents   hang there

someone said tumble
'the sound of words as they tumble
from men's mouths' (or something like that)

there are these areas,
not to be filled, but...

it's a bare canvas, but not empty –
all there under the surface

This is not about writing,
but the whole process
You step off the porch into the dry field
You're there
You see, you're *there*
Now, take it from there...

One, Two, Three

An emperor gives a gift, stylishly,
and a Mughal miniature records it
(colour & gold on paper, height 7 3/16 inches)

we're dazzled   –   all this art
and surprises   'Keeping the doors open'
Right?

Yes, I suppose, fascinated by the delicacy
of the piano part in the first movement
of Beethoven's 'Ghost' Trio
('he sighed…'   but real enough,
aesthetic coat-trailing aside.
The delight beyond the technicalities
– not pursuing, but there
to be recognised

We can see this

 And all those private separations?

When 'we' moves from the general
to the particular?

To talk of *you* now…?
amongst all this 'delight'
– moving into that other level –
the poverty of this, one without the other,
the delight more a refuge than any whole thing
when you're away

Up in the hills the court is assembled,
the gifts exchanged
From the balcony I see you cross a courtyard,
could almost touch you –
but the distance.

             Be well.
the moonlight on your face
as you sleep now

○

hold me

outside the rain falling in the street
I hold you   your flesh so soft

to begin to say – 'I love you…'?

the heat of your belly

away   the hills
(Fuck 'the hills')

my mouth on your throat
my body smells of your body

O

There are many fields
and the fortresses are so far apart.
The troops stand in line on the parade ground
while the sun beats down on them
and their bored officers.

it's another day

meanwhile…

        there are many settings

A group of men can sit stiffly
for a regimental photo of the survivors of the disaster,
and then try to look neat and alert.

And their children…?
living in a calm beyond this knowledge?
It is not so much a question of guilt
on either side, but maybe some form of recognition
which rarely happens.

And the years pass until one generation dies
and their knowledge with them
leaving behind only feelings of confused longing
that quietly spread beyond any conscious resentment.

Now put it together

Blue Enamel Letter J.

the dirt *is* good
Up on the hillsides rocks in the fields –
but ploughed, and sown, and the wheat grows.

At night there are shooting stars
and comets, the moon bright,
but only adding 'weight' to this

We lie together

O

passing through the scattered villages
hill towns in the distance

the touch more than words

years pass   'slowly whittled down,
torn to shreds' – is that the process?
I don't think so, but

that instinct   Always dazzled by the new
and leaving behind something known 'too well'
but not known

the avoidance of these 'difficulties'
a constant despite the 'changes'

The land is rich here,
the terraces of vines and olives

…unable to get this clear,
the process
to live on land the roots growing down
in one place   a movement, yes
but a constant – *that* simplicity

O

The clear blue sky over the mountains reflected
in an enamel miniature portraying exotic scenes with
ornate buildings – The Far East?
'Abandoned temples and palaces set deep in the jungle…'

'things' crowd in   (a fascination with the
forms of obscurity)   then move back
giving you that space around you

It is beyond any conscious decisions, but in the end
involves them
            your kiss

some form of floating

High above the rock outcrops ravens, and hawks
circling   dwelling on one spot
below

New Year

a dark forest somewhere
with a chain of lakes
scattered between the mountains

no one for miles (literally)
except you   a white movement
among the trees   a 'blur'

but more precise than that

maybe a long way off a railway
but I think not
nor a moored seaplane on
one of the lakes

even the possibility of dirt roads
now seems remote

it is all very still
(like) some form of memory
the outline of your breast
seen clothed
in a crowded room

there is the sound of the wind
in the tree tops above you
and your feet on the pine needles below

fading to
the white area in which the 'blur' is lost

the journeys   moving
            '…trying,
to get it right'

that past *now* present
and then…

        we move

not circling but an
unknown progress

looking down the slope
through the trees to the lake
at times losing all sense of direction

now you enter a crowded store
in a large city

it is somehow impassive

'in control'   'our condition'

With a Photo by John Walsh

1

On the maps the countries marked there
and the distances
that separate
the areas between
   ...called 'land masses'

No matter what

You there at that distance
to be measured in miles?

a red truck parked in the dusty town square
here

a relentless and continuing series
of separations that by number grow unreal

left with   the place you're in now
(the word 'you' variable)

From the window

2

the rooms empty   a haze of sunlight
'the dead' pass by?

outside   in the country
the land is rich and fruitful
people hold the harvest with an honest pride
smiling at the camera
the tenderness there of that smile

3

A vegetable market by the roadside
up there   to the north
The station-wagon parked on the gravel

In the room   the silence
dust   caught in a sunbeam
The place like nowhere in its suspension
but everywhere   Again and again

Clouds up over the mountains

        '…part of the process…'

5 Postcards to Alban Berg

1. waves break over the headland
   the pain of closeness / 'to a lover'
   The mountains
   walk in the mountains
   The lightness of touch
   clear air

2. the blue sky
   (pan to) spring ploughing
   and cattle grazing on the (green) slopes
   the wild flowers abundant and   many coloured
   Can you see now?   can I…?
   Many miles away…   Here

3. The dark night   / 'close to your lover'
   the rain and wind outside

4. in the evenings as the sun sets
   red skies and the swimming

   the insult of an image
   when it's only what's here before you

5. the skies clear   (blue)
   midday   the moon still there
   sheep deep in the flowers   daisies and poppies
   Off beyond the distance 'you'
   Minutes in the day when (maybe) the pictures cross
   and focus
   The island   firm
   the mountains up into the sky   'beyond'

'...inside the harm is a clearing...'

1970

'inside the harm is a clearing.........'

There were clouds   the sky was heavy
the rivers were heavy with flood
The line of hills the mud green usual
after the thaw
Through the middle the glint of steel rails
In the valley is a small market town
almost a village

O

In the morning her white body
(it being north european) and the black hairs
Your desire is revived

There comes this desire
to be clean
This involves distance
There comes this decision
of the necessity
in moving
at the right time
in the right way

O

There are many steamers moored in the busy estuary
'Come here'   we lean over the rail
The town is a whole scatter of colours
Our clothes are immaculate and white

The kaleidoscope of the tropics yet the simplicity
As I bend to kiss you my lips brush your hair
Somewhere in the clearing

O

The clutter   Above the ridge
the colours heavy   washed through
and he said then
'every man to his junk-shop'
not moving but fixed
in those same games of 'identity'
Somehow a tight blue blanket
wraps us up
in the silly dreams
Your body

It's never like you dream it
turning this side and that

O

on the edge of town   the scattered houses
the Mill House roaring
people are walking through the water-meadows
it's a mild evening
we're taken in by the very aura
the famous cathedral
and the orchards on the hill-sides
this softness could be in any season

They're like running figures
seen as white flashes in the green distance
towards the rails

◯

'Soon we'll be there   a few more days
you'll like it
the bungalow   the cool verandahs
and our walks in the evening
Naturally my work takes up most of the day
but it's only right that way'

We walk round the deck
the other passengers smile at us kindly
like accomplices in the dream
we all know

As we get under way
a cool breeze comes up river
and ruffles your hair

§ § §

The Big Chop

1969-70

North

Snow on the furrows
and on the hilltop the black castle and cathedral
and the close city like an island
ringed by icy rivers
The days briefer, even darker

>It is the small and isolated fortress
>that lies to the north
>where you are left
>your nakedness on some white winter day

The snow cover
the gardens of ancient houses thick with it
and then the stars

>you know
>we shiver at the contortions
>but have to perform
>the desperate dreams
>that we so carefully build
>in the long weeks of loneliness

>Too cold to even touch the flesh
>yet driven on in the heat of the obsession
>dazed almost when raising the head
>and seeing beyond the window

Split down the middle – what's happening?
The unreality at the wrestling match
and then so much neater to avoid any analysis
with the picture books all ready and the warm fire
The clean white schooner's fascinating voyage

Night Ferry

'The hotels in the narrow side streets…'
appears automatic
and all part of 'the process' whatever that may be

and on the edges of town the sea
and some say the marshes
out of that deep tank of enthusiasm
we all admire so much

being cut in two
kissing round the borders of the hairs
and other reclining positions
back into the personal obscurity
of the obsession
Much grander sounding than when it
comes to crouching naked on all fours
'WOOF'
the animals range away happy as ever

It is the tortuous path threading between
the buildings

'WOOF' (again)

All leading to you and hunger
'I am obsessed with'

But

The travellers leave their bags at the station
and between trains visit the town briefly
It seemed worthless by virtue of its very shallowness
but how to reconcile their journey's necessities
with something nearing any real appreciation?
Can we say 'service'?

Country Diary continued

'Ah, Hilda, my dear, you're so pretty.' (in a German accent)

and the shooting?

I used to shoot a bit in Africa, get a duck or so for supper. But there seemed to be such a lot of killing going on. I felt I could not add to it. I gave up shooting then, except for a little target practice. Lost the taste for it somehow.

'his patrol was ambushed by Zulus'

Today

I tidy the room
it all becomes a notebook or an excuse

> 'A bay seen through the window – it's a
> summer morning – the romantic coaster ploughs on
> leaving a smoky trail behind.
> At sea : 6 bells.'

From the window : cluttered back-yards

It's now down to a matter of lists
that act as buttresses, even defences.
No? the same tired and selfish stories?

Out there...

There seems to be great activity
and everyone has been invited to collaborate
It's all very curious and useless
I mean 'what body winds round what body?'
a poor excuse for 'intellectual search'
or 'a full and active life' –
though at times being 'in love' is a life in itself

The floor is swept and all the ledges meticulously dusted
the room is then well aired by opening the window wide
I'm left standing in the middle of the room
holding a wet cloth

There are too many accounts of cruelties
but the other side always sounds slightly false
or is an expression of nostalgia
But what can ache more than repetition?

Cut into slices?
Stuck in *'the vertical'* – is that too obscure?

S... – Hebrew for 'Beautiful'

the night is soft
I give in   it is warm
you're not far away
but somehow suspended in the distance

I trail behind me many failings
that invade too much of what we are
'Forgive me' is very weak

The animals at the zoo were very grand
I admired them
and the gardens so heavy and green
You must see so much
that you let pass   to turn in welcome

Brooklyn

The city isn't necessary to our elegance
It's not a matter of going back
to the land
but *that kiss* on the forehead

The wind is so strong and yet soft
almost tender
At night on the ferry – the lights of passing tugs and freighters
It is hard, I know, to live without this,
'out of love' as they say.
What can I say?   we kiss
with all the need and hope that
comes from this 'lack'

You are beautiful   the whiteness of your breasts

We have this

Little Lord Fauntleroy Meets the Secret Garden

Nanny will look after the boy –
a new rocking horse *has* been installed in the nursery
Meanwhile, after our little walk, my butler
will bring us tea on the lawn

The sea was very rough today
but the waves *were* exciting, weren't they

'I can keep this up for hours, you know'

Meanwhile back on the lawn everything is very calm
and dazzlingly peaceful
You eat the little sandwiches with such elegance
You're not what I call a truly graceful person
with not the least suggestion of the self-conscious
in fact you're wide-eyed

Next we imagine what elegant rats we'd make
walking through Brighton with out tails stylishly slung over our arms

§ § §

H. M. S. "FURIOUS". Mediterranean Squadron.

H.M.S. Blue Flag

1967-68

The Situation

'Dear Doctor…'   So many…   Galileo…
and all the worlds in The World and his telescope was now useless
At the beginning of a story there are so many raised hopes
This letter began 'You've been too kind'

The empty country house burst into song with
'O sinner-man, where you gonna run to?'
But by now so many of the fine gauze screens
had been broken through and it became only too evident
that the 'good' people were not so good
and that 'Goodness' was still an ideal which no one had realised.
The gardens all gone to seed, and nobody's fault, though…

And in 'Timothy's Space Book' there's no mention
of the monk Copernicus. Everything seems wrong.
The gardens all gone to seed and in the last
crudely coloured picture the returned astronaut waves
a *handkerchief* from the capsule's door.
The grounds so vast and in the middle of all this
the house. It had all been allowed to deteriorate
without stop, until it had gone beyond the point
of any easy or simple remedies. Now the whole operation
would have to be both drastic and costly, if at all.

'The prison of images pursuing, with beautiful
women, the hero of the ritual.' That was another story.
History had to be forgotten with so much work at hand.

So far, you see, there can be nothing but confusion
and misappellation, which in turn causes a neglect
now only too evident. To ask for forgiveness is absurd.

If he named a dark dream 'the sea of honey',
then why not go on?   though with the reservation
that perhaps there are too many words.

An ancient freighter painted black and red
blew her sirens as she left the dock and steamed
slowly down river to the sea.
You can now add this to the list of symbols
already provided – the large house and the boy's 'Space Book'.
Yes, it brings us all back to 'the beginning'
and 'the confusion' again. Yet, in fact, each is a separate
world, despite repetition blurring the edges.
'You've been too kind' is your world, and
it is not vanity, only time, that makes me
say yours is the simpler one at present,
while mine is the reverse, through my own fault,
with all escape routes blocked and trapped;
the group of viciously conflicting emotions and fears causing
a general inability to cope, to say the least.
Is it surprising – this retreat into the house
and a mass of trivial details?
But as this is too neatly explained, the question of
the 'wrongness' and 'good' stand out even more
as remaining unanswered.
Even a retreat has to end somewhere.

You will not be surprised if I leave now.
To stay longer would only…
More words would be useless.   Our talk…
'Forgive me, you're too kind' – with such clumsiness
and a self-disgust that embarrassed everyone.
So let's let the ship sail through the house.
Forget the 'Space Book'.
It doesn't matter.
'Dear Doctor, the pain…'   If even the exit could be graceful
and nothing else, then…
All escape routes blocked   The undergrowth so thick
'A matter of time'

Dawn of the Monsters

The sky grows pale with dawn
the birds sing there – maybe only three or four distinct songs –
but with more clarity in this than anywhere else
At this hour the sky is a soft blur
with black silhouettes on the horizon and pale stars
scattered – no one caring if they do move

In a different town far from here…
I'm not sure why I should be aware of you
– a common 'wretchedness'?
more imagined than real? You forgive me
there's nothing else to do   'I give in.'

Paleness soaks deeper and deeper into the atmosphere
like an admission of collapse where nothing is touched

Chemical Days

'The fix' can only mean
the man with two blue flags who stands all day
on the cliff top. Now he's waving them at
the aircraft-carrier, H.M.S. Blue Flag, that is
as hard and clumsy as most machines.
This process is called an 'euphemism'.
The wars, fathers, spacemen, soldiers –
just so many toys to be broken or dismembered.
Even the flag man and his strange obsession…
What there is…   I mean, couldn't it really be
a matter of compasses like fixing the sun or
the stars, or the hour for the 'fix'?
This process is called a 'smoke screen'.
When it's raining and the isolation of the day
can only mean 'the fix' or a studied chaos
of words and pictures in the hope of distraction
or, even weaker yet more honest, justification
for existence. Tears are so much of the past.
'Shall I have them all shot?
or just the leaders? That's quite a question.'
Click! went the heels. A door banged in the yard.
Blue flags fluttering – 'What's happening?'
It was all there waiting – a complete change of lives
– why the delay? Courage wasn't even
relevant, only 'common sense' for a change.
She was still waiting in the yard patiently.
Everyone acknowledged her beauty and love.
'this stupidity'

The Revisitation

Despite the dazzle of the New
– its own great and unique beauty –
(her long black hair reflecting a summer morning)
when the past's too roughly torn away
you can't deny the deep pain that
runs the length of my body
like the crack from an earthquake
that splits the new tarmac road
right down the middle for half a mile
Plate 56 in your geography text book
Its ragged lips have already tasted death many times
An equatorial republic asking for aid
a large ship at anchor in the sound
a new pipe-line and harbour installations
the black capstan

(As a footnote – the escape was made
through a slim steel pipe which even you must know)
and that's enough said for now

Yet with this there is certainly no reason
for bitterness or resentment – they have no part in this.
In fact there is nothing but the endurance,
there's not even a neat conclusion or clichéd saying
to draw on for cheap comfort –
only time and the inevitable process of a darkening memory.
No one can be truly put at ease by this
as such inconclusiveness is always discomforting

The poem can always retreat
into an elaboration of the tropical scene
mentioned before, and time is passing
for all of us – isn't it?

Which island was it that the schooner
visited that year…

Dazzle

       the dazzle of the New
– its own great and unique beauty –
(her long black hair reflecting a summer morning)
like the fresh white liner at anchor
in the sparkling blue sound of this Pacific island

An equatorial republic asking for foreign aid –
the large ship at anchor; a new pipe-line
and harbour installations; the glossy black capstan
and tar melting on the roads.
So many excuses and subsequent apologies
for the numerous blunders and inefficiencies
of my native workers –
the covers and symbols of my own astonishment
and love for you

But still I can't stop this wonder
that dumbfounds me every time I see you,
or, when alone, ever come to a full realisation
of what's happened and is still happening
and will continue happening.

I just gape at you
and know how I must appear so crazy
all red faced and sweating in the ridiculous
general's uniform of my small republic.
I am weighed down with gold braid,
epaulettes, medals, swords and nonsense,
as you pass in a light summer dress.

Forestry Work no. 1

Did I say that?
The prospect of such expanses still to be covered…
hardly having set out   intimidated   so soon?
Up onto the ridge   the forest here like a cool grove of ash
with sunlight filtering down
Like a pilgrimage, maybe?
On the map there are a series of points   'The Procession'
Later playing with the children, it's quite natural…
Your body gives   'The Acceptance'

I pick the wild flowers carefully
and take exactly one example of each species
'and with reeds and yellow marsh flowers in the clearing'
This conscious and essential 'delicacy' in handling surroundings,
of course, flows out   takes in the
You understand this when we touch

In turn I slow my instincts   I know
to take in all the marvels as you give them me
So many pictures of 'The Dreams'

Love in the Organ Loft

The cathedral lay feeling rather damp among its trees
and lawns, lichen covering its white stone walls
near the ground that is still wet from a rain shower.
It is April – of course. (Why should songs have all
the good lines? – like 'I love you', too.)

I'm beginning to wonder what I'm doing
and what is going on? All I know is that it's now
very late at night, or early in the morning…
You see, even this is disturbing and disordered.
Is someone weeping in the street outside?
It sounds like a man. It is 3.30 a.m.
But when I go to the window, I can see no one.
I might have asked him in to cry in the warm,
if he'd wanted. This isn't as stupid as it seems.
But everything on this (surface) level is so disjointed
that it can make even this possible act of kindness
appear to 'THEM' as 'foolishness' (if 'they' feel patronising)
or 'absurdity' (if 'they' feel insecure that day).

At 5.00 a.m. I am still watching over my love
– I love her more, so much more, than I've ever loved anyone,
even myself. In fact, this is a completely new
experience of *love*, like it is the first REAL time,
and love for real.
            'My eyes hurt now, but birds begin
to sing outside anticipating the dawn – though I can find
no connection. Why should I? How absurd can I get
in this county town of the south-west province?
There appear to be no limits anywhere anymore.'
'His lips were sealed.' 'What is going on now?
You needn't doubt that I'll just wait –
'Faites vos jeux' – until I get to the bottom of this.'

The cathedral and its own lush green and garden,
and the comfortable and quietly rich church houses

with their private gardens that are set out
around the green – they are all peaceful and certain.
There is no question of escapism. (And it's about time
I woke up to this fact and appreciated the possible
sincerity of many such people and bodies.)

The birds masquerading as a 'dawn chorus'
have now become quite deafening with their twitterings
– I am sending for a shot-gun sales catalogue.

But what can this mean? – that I should
sit here all night watching over my love
and at the same time I fix
more than double my usual intake
to feel without compassion my brain wince
under chemical blows.

I mean what is happening? – NOW!   Do you see
what I mean? – like does the cathedral nestle
in the sky's warm lap? *OR* does the sky
respectfully arch over the cathedral's gothic
towers and roof, flying buttresses and pinnacles?
This parable can be used for most things – think of a river...

The belief that ignorance is usually cloaked
in pompous wordiness seems well proven
by everything put down so far. And, in fact,
anyone feeling the need to relieve his by now strong
resentment of me will be, when possible,
met in all humility. I accept my guilt
and am not surprised at these numerous 'accidents'
that seem to follow my progress through this city,
like falling slates and flower pots.

But please, when you all feel relieved,
will someone tell me how it is I am
so blessed at last with a real love
– and this like I've never seen possessed by anyone?
But also...   and yet...

And yet I know I need no explanations
and, least of all, justifications. The fact that the woman
I love with such continual and intense joy
and find what was before always transitory
an eternal and unshakeable happiness. All this
is this is this is this...   I'm so happy;
and now as she turns in her sleep
her face's beauty fills me with a tenderness
and adoration that surprises even me, and fills my eyes with happy tears.

It's 6.00, and with the morning light
it seems my guard is over. No one comes
to relieve me – I couldn't stand rivals.
But why is the morbid masochism
of lines 46 to 47 still around? – Has it
no sense of decorum? All I want is to be able to
love as I'm loved and make my love happy.
Nobody here wants jack-boots,
or sleek vicious cars, or sleek vicious lovers,
or cocktail cabinets that play 'Jingle Bells'
every time you open the doors – 'Oh boy!'.
All we want is ourselves – and that *is* really great.

But, please, if anyone has any answers
to the little problem of diet, do tell me.
I must go to bed now, but messages
can always be safely left here. Goodnight.
Good morning.
            The cathedral is so pretty
here, especially in spring – so do visit.

Exeter. April 1967.
for Marian

The Nine Death Ships

1

'This isn't the Black Forest!' he cried. But the sky was *so* blue.

'Do come in and put your revolver on the sideboard.' And so, many days passed. It all became very neat and tidy. The house was swept clean and all the revolvers put in a drawer suitably labelled.

'I'm getting closer.'

'You sure are.'

2

The three men were very persistent, to the extent that they even became boring. The servants were appropriately informed. Only the dogs looked glum at the new situation.

'BANG!' – that changed it.

'My sweet, you see what I mean?'

The carriage continued ignoring the man who quietly read a newspaper.

3

Manhattan is not at all confusing if one appreciates logic. I do, for one.

4

The little house was so full of people that inevitably one of the walls gave way – but, surprisingly, nobody was injured or upset in the least.

'What a magnificent garden you have!'

We lolled the whole afternoon.

It was impossible to count the number of woodpeckers in the flock. But, unperturbed, they continued to wreck the country's entire telegraphic system.

The shot-gun blasted away.

5

'My eyes hurt from doing so much finely detailed clerical work in such a badly lit office.'

That was how the report began.

Death was so near, it became a shy joke among the inmates.

6

There was a small black book on the well scrubbed table in the lighthouse. You could hear the sea pounding the walls outside. Inside the book were stuck several photographs of gravestones in wintery graveyards. It was late winter. There were also some postcards which portrayed the deaths of various characters. One was an obvious choice – 'The Death of Chatterton' – painted by Henry Wallis. But the oval photo of Miller was not at all expected. The caption simply said 'MILLER / Northfield Bank Robber / Killed on front of Bank, Sept. 1876.' He lay naked and dead on the mortuary slab. The photo shows only his head, shoulders, chest and upper-arms. There were two obvious bullet holes – one low in his left shoulder, and the other high in the middle of his forehead. But it was only the first wound that had a stream of blood running from it.

The noise of the storm had by now grown quite deafening. It was impossible to hear what anyone said, no matter how loud they shouted. I was then further upset by the discovery that I was alone in the lighthouse. And it didn't look as though anyone would ever return. It was not even known if there had been anyone there to leave in the first place. It was all very confusing, and it seemed that I never would meet the owner of the small black book. For the while he certainly showed no intentions of returning for it.

I carried on whittling and putting ships in bottles.

Spring ploughing would be our next worry.

7

The houses were all yellow and the ladders green – such a conscious plan of life and its colours could only be described as 'revolting', and that was being too kind by far.

The lush red of blood, though, and all its varying moods and hues was a continual source of surprise and joy.

'Don't worry.'

8

'It was raining so hard and all the games had been played. There was nothing for it – we would just have to spend the afternoon watching the servants play leapfrog. What a bore.'

Luckily he never finished his memoirs.

9

It seemed that the worst was over. The iron black fleet had finally steamed out of the bay. There was no communication. But at dawn the horizon was still empty. The sea was slate grey. If only this had been 'the worst' – but nobody can tell. The year was unsure – maybe it was 1900 or 1901.

The orchestra had to be slaughtered – they put everyone's nerves on edge. It was only through luck that Stravinsky escaped. That would be funnier if it was a joke. Insanity is always terrifying and illogical in its own logic.

As a distraction, let's not forget 'the amusing woodpeckers' or 'the surprising shot-gun' or 'the confusing yet simple street map of Manhattan'. They all serve some purpose – whatever that is.

A NOTE BY THE AUTHOR

This collection was written between 1967 and 1972. The work really has its seeds in my book *The White Room* (1968), and also is where *The Sinking Colony* (1970) left off, even though some of the work here was written at the same time as the work in that book, and a few poems even before that time. (I want to state here my sense of this continuity.) It is a development from there – towards a greater complexity, and range. Not only containing varied information, but having an energy and necessity as well. The two qualities – presentation of information and the art as mover, catalyst – to somehow work together, be one.

The collection is set out to be seen the way you see a plant. It begins with the sequence, 'The Long Black Veil', the end-product, the "flower" of my work to date, and then moves on down to the origins, the roots of that work, the earlier poems and the poems written at the same time as I was writing 'The Long Black Veil'. The whole book is one crystal in which things ricochet back and forth, echo and re-echo. In which light enters and bounces out again changed in form and direction. And the crystal itself alive and growing.

(The above appeared on the front jacket flap of the 1975 edition.)

A Note from the Publisher

This volume is part of a series that is devoted to recovering out-of-print volumes that – in my view – should be made available again. The books date from the 1970s to the 2000s and all of the first dozen volumes have been important to me in one way or another. Most are long out of print, although some can be found within subsequent collected editions.

HMS Little Fox was an important volume in Lee Harwood's career, his first significant full-length collection after the trio of fine Fulcrum Press volumes (*The White Room, Landscapes* and *The Sinking Colony*), and won the Poetry Society's Alice Hunt Bartlett Prize in 1976. The book was published by my old friend, the late Ian Robinson, at his Oasis Books imprint in 1975, and marked a new phase in the author's work, especially the opening sequence, *The Long Black Veil*, although this was not ultimately to be a direction that his work would often take.

The text and presentation here follows the original, albeit not slavishly. Some minor typos have been corrected, but things that were changed by the author for the poems' later appearance in the *Collected Poems* (Shearsman Books, 2004) have been left as they were in the original, as the intention is to reflect the first edition, not the author's later thoughts. It should be noted that one poem here, 'Little Lord Fauntleroy Meets the Secret Garden', was excluded by the author from the *Collected*.

I am grateful to Robert Sheppard, executor of Lee Harwood's literary estate, for his assistance in the preparation of this volume.

Tony Frazer
September 2018

www.ingramcontent.com/pod-product-compliance
Lightning Source LLC
Chambersburg PA
CBHW030909170426
43193CB00009BA/783